Paintball 101 ™

Paintball From The Basics to Starting a Tournament Team

by Larry Sekely

About the Book

Paintball 101 explains the basics of the game of paintball form the beginning to forming your own tournament team, written at a level that newer players will be able to easily grasp. This book is primarily an overview of the game, touching on topics from getting started to the various styles of the game, basic strategies and basic paintball plays. The book also goes into detail on what to expect the first time you walk on to a paintball field, what the typical costs may be and how to prepare so that your first experience is an enjoyable one.

This book will also provides a brief explanation and comparison on some of the paintball gear along with the authors' impressions on what he considers to be the best choices for certain styles of play.

In addition, the book addresses common mistakes by newer players as well as basic skills that newer players need to constantly work on to become better.

For those players who want to take their game to the next level, the book also explains how to organize and start a tournament paintball team and enjoy competitive paintball at least at a local level.

The author wishes to acknowledge the following individuals for their role in producing this book.

Interior Layout and design

Colleen Mackin
Colleenm@tampabay.rr.com

Cover photography

Joshua D. Silverman
www.Joshuasilverman.com

Executive consultant

Jason Sekely

Artistic consultant

Jessica Sekely

Note for Librarians: A cataloguing record for this book is available from Library and Archives Canada at www.collectionscanada.ca/amicus/index-e.html
ISBN 1-4120-7133-x

Printed in Victoria, BC, Canada. Printed on paper with minimum 30% recycled fibre. Trafford's print shop runs on "green energy" from solar, wind and other environmentally-friendly power sources.

TRAFFORD™
PUBLISHING™

Offices in Canada, USA, Ireland and UK
This book was published *on-demand* in cooperation with Trafford Publishing. On-demand publishing is a unique process and service of making a book available for retail sale to the public taking advantage of on-demand manufacturing and Internet marketing. On-demand publishing includes promotions, retail sales, manufacturing, order fulfilment, accounting and collecting royalties on behalf of the author.

Book sales for North America and international:
Trafford Publishing, 6E–2333 Government St.,
Victoria, BC v8t 4p4 CANADA
phone 250 383 6864 (toll-free 1 888 232 4444)
fax 250 383 6804; email to orders@trafford.com
Book sales in Europe:
Trafford Publishing (UK) Limited, 9 Park End Street, 2nd Floor
Oxford, UK oxi 1hh UNITED KINGDOM
phone 44 (0)1865 722 113 (local rate 0845 230 9601)
facsimile 44 (0)1865 722 868; info.uk@trafford.com
Order online at:
trafford.com/05-2028

10 9 8 7 6 5 4

This book is not derived from, nor connected with the regular department entitled "Paintball 101" which appears in Paintball Magazine
(www.paintballmag.com)

Paintball 101

Paintball From The Basics To Starting a Tournament Team

By Larry Sekely

Table of Contents

 **Contents**

Contents

ACKNOWLEDGEMENTS

For Barbara, my lovely wife, who supported me all of these years when I was gone for days at a time, attending World Cup, playing in a tournament, or practicing with my team. She would come and watch me play tournaments whenever she could. At the Tampa NPPL Tournament in May 2005, I recall looking up and seeing her sitting in the stands with my daughter cheering us on. It was such a great feeling.

For my daughter, Jessica, who, when I came back from the field, always wanted to see how many bruises I had. She would count them one at a time. Poor Daddy. (I would encourage her to stop counting after seven.)

And for my son, Jason, who was the one that actually introduced me to the sport after attending a friends birthday outing at a local Paintball field. When his mother and I came to pick him up he said, "Dad, you've got to try this. It's soooo cool!" I know now, of course, that part of his motivation to get me involved was that he would get to play more often and I would also fund him getting the proper equipment. Smart kid. I have many fond memories of him and I playing paintball together these past six years, from the day he got his first marker to the day I watched him play a one on three in the semi finals of a local tournament and pull off the win.

To Tim, Alicia, and Bernie Altman, owners and operators of Gator Paintball Extreme in Hudson, Florida. These individuals do an incredible job of attending to the needs of several hundred paintball enthusiasts each and every weekend. They successfully cater to first time players, scenario players, woods players, and tournament players alike. Tim offers coaching and advice and encourages players to take their game to the next level and was instrumental in helping me form my first team. Many local teams as well as rec ball players call Gator Paintball their home.

<u>INTRODUCTION</u>

I remember the first time I went to play paintball at the local field. I felt lost. I knew that I wanted to go out and shoot em up and have fun, but I had no clue about how to play the game. There had to be more to it than hiding behind a prop and popping up every now and then to shoot my marker. I really wanted to get involved in the game, but how do you go about learning the basics?

Well, that is exactly what *Paintball 101* is all about....the basics.....the first step....the introductory course.

I want to convey what I have learned over the years to those individuals just starting out, in the hopes of being able to help them develop their game faster. In addition, this book is meant to be an information source that younger players can share with their parents to help ease any concerns or apprehension they may have. I also want to be able to help players form their own competitive teams by offering them tips on how to get started, how to get organized, skills that need to be learned and some basic paintball plays to run as your team grows.

I hope that reading this book will help you enjoy the sport of paintball even more.

DEDICATION

In Memory of Christopher Hidalgo

Chris was only 14 years old at the time of his death in a tragic drowning accident on July 5, 2004. He had long since been a paintball enthusiast and was associated with several local teams prior to him joining my son, Jason, several other local players and myself to form Team ICE. These young players all shared a passion for the sport and quickly developed as one of strongest teams in the area, placing second in tournaments in Miami, Port Canaveral, and Tampa.

Chris was the co-captain, of the team and a born leader. He coordinated most of the team's schedule and had a superb knowledge of markers and equipment. He had aspirations of opening his own paintball shop. His untimely death was a real shock to his teammates. We were in the middle of a three part series tournament at that time and firmly held second place.

Chris's mother, Tammy, requested that the team attend his funeral dressed in their paintball uniforms and conduct a military style salute with their paintball markers. Chris was buried in full paintball attire.

We miss you, Chris.

Your spirit and your love of the game will always be a part of us.

Chapter One
Paintball at a Glance
What is Paintball?

Paintball is a game that combines the elements of "Tag" and "Hide and Seek" into one. When you are "tagged", it is by a paintball shot out of a paintball marker (also called a paintball gun). It is a game that is very intense at times and, with all the latest technology in markers, very sophisticated.

A paintball is a .68 caliber gelatin capsule filled with non-toxic, non-caustic, biodegradable, colored liquid fill.

The paintball is propelled out of an air powered (CO_2 or high pressure air) marker at speeds of up to 300 FPS (Feet Per Second). When a paintball "hits" you or any part of your equipment and breaks, leaving a splat the diameter of a quarter or larger, you are said to be "marked" or "hit" and therefore eliminated from the game.

The colored fill should wash out of clothes with water and normal everyday laundry detergent. When paintball first started, the fill inside the balls was oil based, which would require the players to use turpentine to clean up.

Remember playing cowboys and Indians when we were kids? How about combat or even war? Characteristically, men and boys alike have always had a fascination for guns. How about the Red Rider BB rifle in the movie "A Christmas Story?"

The attraction of paintball to me is obvious. As human beings, we have a basic "warrior" instinct and a competitive nature. Although it may be more prevalent in males than females, we still all possess these characteristics. That is why sporting events are so popular throughout the world for both participants and spectators. It's the thrill of the hunt. It's the fast paced action, blood pumping, heart stopping adrenaline rush that makes paintball one of the top extreme sports today.

It is also a team sport. Your victories or defeats will be based on how well you play as a team in addition to your own individual abilities.

Talk to any pro team and they will tell you that communicating positions of your opponents, coordinating moves up the field and playing well as a team will make you more successful. This is the reason many corporations and church groups have regular paintball outings to build teamwork and camaraderie.

There are many different ways the game itself can be played. Players are normally divided into two teams; the number of players on each team can vary depending on the format of that specific game. The object of a typical game of "capture the flag" is to advance down the field (eliminating opponents along the way) and capture your opponents' flag while protecting yours.

Paintball game variations are limited only by the imaginations of the field owners or the players themselves.

Paintball is Growing

Since its inception in 1981, the sport of paintball has grown at a phenomenal rate. Amercian Sports Data, Inc. started tracking paintball in 1998. The breakdown of those figures until now are as follows:

YEAR	PARTICIPANTS IN MILLIONS
1989	Under 1 million
1999	5.9
2000	6.3
2001	7.1
2002	8.7
2003	9.8

Footnote: Action Pursuit Games Magazine, September 2004, American Sports Data, Inc. Outdoor Activities 1999, as reported by the Sporting Goods Manufacturer Association.

♦ These numbers represent a growth in our sport of an amazing 66% in just 5 years and a 13.3% growth from 2002 to 2003 alone.

♦ Paintball is classified as an extreme sport by the SGMA and is ranked third in that category behind inline skating and skateboarding.

♦ It is interesting to note that from 2002 to 2003, inline skating dropped 10.8% in participation and skateboarding dropped 14.7% while paintball increased 13.3%.

12

- Paintball has more participants than wakeboarding, roller hockey, rock climbing, windsurfing and mountain climbing combined.

- 85% of frequent paintball players are male. Nearly 90% of frequent paintball players are between the ages of 12 & 24 with the average age being 20.

- 4.6% is in the 35-44 age bracket and the 45-54 ages grew to 4.7%.

- The 55-64 age bracket has just entered the market at .4%.

- 41% of all frequent players live in the South while 35% live in the North Central part of the United States.

- The overall number for paintball participation in 2004 is easily expected to surpass the 10 million mark and, if trends continue, may be the #2 extreme sport within a couple of years.

Paintball Popularity

The sport of paintball is getting more exposure and growing in popularity at an incredible rate. When I first started playing paintball, I would engage in conversation with friends or associates at work about how each others weekend went and what did you do yadda, yadda, yadda. When I mentioned that I had played paintball on Saturday, I would get all kinds of various reactions from, "You did what?" or "What's paintball?" to "I've heard about that!" Inevitably, this would lead into detailed explanation about what the sport is all about.

Today, when the topic comes up, I am constantly surprised at not only how many people are aware of paintball, but how many of these individuals have played it themselves or had sons, daughters or friends that have played the game.

Paintball is becoming increasingly more visible on television. The game has been featured on shows such as *King of Queens*, *Fear Factor*, *CSI Miami*, *Gilmore Girls*, *My Big Fat Obnoxious Boss*... just to name a few. Unfortunately, some of the scenes depicted on T.V. did not emphasize the degree of safety that playing the sport requires, such as the proper use of paintball goggles. However, it is interesting to see how mainstream paintball is becoming.

As of this writing, *Spike T.V.* has a 30 minute segment every Saturday morning at 9:00A.M. covering paintball tournaments, scenario games and the like.

At the 2004 World Cup Tournament held at the Disney Wide World of Sports Complex in Orlando, Florida, Dick Clark himself, gave a presentation on his plans to bring competitive paintball to televison. ESPN filmed the 2004 World Cup to be shown on T.V.

William Shatner of Star Trek fame has led the Federation forces in major scenario games called *Splatt Attack*, an annual paintball extravaganza with proceeds going to charity.

George Clooney and Will Smith, are each reported to have their own paintball teams.

Perhaps one of the most prominent paintball celebrities was the late Maurice Gibb of the Bee Gees. "Commander Mo" as he was known in the paintball circle, was the team captain of the Royal Rat Rangers. He also opened a first rate paintball shop in Miami, Florida called Commander Mo's.

I had the distinct pleasure of meeting him briefly at the 2001 World Cup. I was waiting to watch his team play when I approached him for a picture with my son. He was very cordial to us.

We ran into him again at the 2002 World Cup when I said, "Hi Captain Mo!" He stopped, said hello and sat down with us for a moment to chat. A finer person you would never meet. The NPPL (National Professional Paintball League) hosts the Commander's Cup Tournament each year in his honor. He will be sorely missed by his fans in both the music and paintball industry.

Commander Mo and Jason

Chapter Two
Styles and Fields

If the idea of running around and shooting at people is appealing, but you don't know what the games are all about, you are not alone. Many individuals are unaware of the many styles of paintball that are played today. They range from sneaking and sniping to fast paced and rapid fire. Which style will appeal most to you depends on many factors. Your age, physical dexterity, how often you want to play as well as how much you are willing to invest, may all have a bearing on which style of paintball is best suited for you. However, it may simply boil down to what it is you want to do. In this chapter, the various styles of play are described along with the different fields of play.

Rec Ball

Rec ball is a generic term used to describe the style of play that is utilized by the recreational paintballer. These individuals may or may not play regularly, but come out on a weekend, maybe with a couple of friends, to have some fun. The style of games that they will play will be determined by the field refs, but will usually rotate to all the games the field has to offer. Many fields have tournament teams that come out regularly to practice on the airball or hyperball fields. These players are normally segregated from rec ballers because of their level of skill.

17

The refs will call all rec ballers together and divide them up into two teams. They will make sure all players have read the mandatory rules and had the safety briefing before any games begin. In addition, they will review the rules of the field to be played on, answer any last minute questions and get the games started. At the conclusion of the game, players will have enough time to air up and load up before reporting for the next game. Normally, each game will be played on a different field randomly throughout the day.

Woods Games

Played in the woods on the natural terrain, the size of the fields vary. Bunkers are usually set up as a stack of logs, small plywood bunkers, old fences, barrels, forts, foxholes and anything else from the imagination of the field owners. Players often wear a variety of camo clothing as this is a game of hide and seek in the woods. Teams start at opposite ends of the fields and slowly and stealthily advance through the woods eliminating opponents along the way.

Attack and Defend

A variation of a woods game, there is typically a large fort or other structure at one end of the field or perhaps at the top of a hill. One team will be placed inside the fort to defend it. They may or may not be permitted at any time during the game to leave the structure. The other team moves through the woods and sneaks up and attacks the fort attempting to eliminate the players inside. The team inside the fort tries to eliminate their opponents as they approach the fort.

Scenario Games

Scenario games are fast growing in popularity. These games are perfect for players that want more out of paintball than just capturing flags and shooting and eliminating other players.

All scenario games have a theme involving role playing or re-enactment of a historical battle or event. Players take on new identities, wear uniforms or costumes. They can become Generals and go on missions, achieve objectives to earn points for prizes. Often prizes are given for the best costumes. Players may also use paintgrenades or paintmines depending on the rules of that particular game.

These games can go on continuously for 48 to 72 hours. Many players camp out at the field and grab what rest they can between missions.

One of the most popular organizers of scenario games is Wayne Dollack of Wayne's World of Paintball in Ocala, Florida. He is well known for hosting some of the most elaborate and well organized games in the country.

Speedball

Speedball is a style of play that is designed for action and played on a specific size field. Speedball fields are usually set up in an open field with little or no natural cover. Bunkers are man-made and symmetrically placed on both halves of the field, or mirrored so that neither team has any advantage over the other due to the layout.

The bunkers may be configured such that they have to be played from a kneeling position or maneuvered through by crawling on your stomach. Some bunkers can be played from a stand up position. These fields are normally set up for 5, 7 or 10 man play.

When "Game On" is called, all players break for their starting bunkers in a flurry of paint. Both teams are constantly shooting paint while advancing down field and trying to eliminate opponents. Games played on a speed ball field are very fast paced, and last only 3 to 12 minutes depending on the size of the teams.

Hyperball Field

Hyperball is speedball played on a field with bunkers made out of large plastic drain pipes. The bunkers vary in size from large to small in height and width. There are usually only a couple of stand ups. Often there will be an "X" or "octopus" at the center fifty with numerous "lay downs", "choo-choos" and perhaps even a "snake".

Airball Field

Airball fields use air filled blow up bunkers of numerous shapes and sizes. Most all large tournaments are played on this type of field because they are very versatile and easy to set up. These bunkers allow players to tuck in and play tight. Players will actually push in the sides of the bunkers with their barrels to provide as much protection for themselves as possible.

20

Field owners use the versatility of airball bunkers to change the layouts often to achieve a new look and make the game a little more challenging for their regular players .

X Ball

X Ball is a tournament style of paintball played on a airball field utilizing an almost hockey-like format. X Ball was developed to be more spectator friendly and this format also makes it more suitable for TV.

It is a multi-match competition set up with two 20 minute halves. The objective of the game is to hang the flag as often as possible before the time runs out. Each flag hang marks the end of the game, the beginning of a two minute "pit stop"and then a new game. During the "pit stop", players will have two minutes to air up, refill pods, clean off hits and be ready to start the next game. Substitutions can be made at this time.

Penalties are assessed for infractions such as two minutes for playing on with an unobvious hit, four minutes for playing on with an obvious hit and, and ten minutes for a major fraction such as an illegal marker. The guilty player will serve his time in the "penalty box" and his team will have to continue to play with one man short.

One difference in X Ball is that each team has a coach assigned to the coach's box at the sideline at midfield. He calls out opponents' positions and tells the players on his team when to move. There are also additional sideline coaches outside of the main field of play that direct players and call out positions as well, sometimes utilizing signs to communicate to the players on the field.

If a game is about to be lost, that teams' coach can "throw in the towel" which automatically gives the win to the other team, but stops the clock. This tactic can be beneficial under certain circumstances.

Other than these differences, the actual games themselves are very similar to five man play. In this format, however, losing one game doesn't hurt a team nearly as much as in a regular tournament due to the number of actual games played.

X Ball is very fast, very intense, and a lot of fun to watch.

Chapter Three
Safety in Paintball

Many uninformed individuals mistakenly feel that paintball is a "dangerous" sport that promotes violence and vandalism. To me, paintball is a game that is a tremendous amount of fun to play. I will probably continue to play the sport until I am no longer physically able.

When playing at the local paintball fields, safety is paramount. If a player breaks one of the fields rules, he or she is given a stern warning. If there is a second infraction, the player is required to sit out the next game. Should there be a third offense, the player is required to leave the field for the rest of the day. This practice is commonplace for most fields that I have played on over the years. In addition, the more experienced players assist the field refs by re-enforcing the rules and looking after the newer players.

I have personally introduced the game to many individuals, some of which have gone on to become regular players. I still ref for private parties, birthdays and corporate outings. Many church groups throughout the country play paintball as a means of promoting fellowship. Paintball is less violent than football, basketball, hockey or soccer, to name just a few. If you were to condone paintball because of the danger or the aggressiveness of play, then you would have to first condone most organized sports that are played today. At least in paintball there are no injuries from bodies crashing into one another (usually anyway). No physical contact is allowed in paintball.

The game, by nature, promotes teamwork. Whether you are a woods, tournament, scenario or rec ball player it involves working with and relying on your teammates to achieve a common goal- winning the game. Yes, it is a game and those of us that have played paintball for years keep that in perspective. Sure, you are going to have those days when you get deliberately shot after calling yourself out or you see a player "playing on" (cheating) with an obvious hit. These things are inevitably going to happen on occasion. As in any other competitive sport, there will be differences of opinions, arguments and emotional flare ups. All players need to strive to keep their emotions under control and in check and keep the fun in the game.

The key safety rules are as follows:

Safety Briefing

This is normally given by the owner, head ref, or another field designate. The purpose of this briefing is to make all players familiar with safety rules, regulations and penalties for infractions for this particular field. This meeting is mandatory for all players to the field prior to any play.

Barrel Plugs/Barrel Socks

These are to remain on the markers at all times except in an authorized shooting area. Removals are permitted only at the ref's direction.

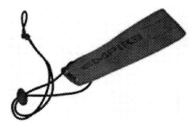

Goggles

Approved paintball masks/goggles_must be worn at all times upon entering the field of play and not removed again until returning to the staging area. There are other areas at the field where goggles are required to be worn such as the chrono station,_target range, or the paths to a woods game or any other location as deemed necessary by the field owners. In certain weather conditions, goggles can fog up. Should this happen, remove yourself from the field for your safety as well as the safety of others. You must without exception, wear your goggles when on the field. No matter if you have to sneeze, blow chunks or a bee flies under your mask, <u>keep the goggles on</u>!

Chrono Station

A chronograph measures the speed a ball travels as it leaves the marker. All players are required to chrono their markers each day prior to playing their first game. The maximum setting cannot exceed 300 FPS (Feet Per Second). Fields vary on their maximum settings anywhere from 275 FPS to 300 FPS (or even lower at indoor fields) depending on where you play. If you have ever been shot by a "hot marker", you know how important this safety rule is. It is advisable to

(and many fields do this automatically) chrono before each game and at mid-day. The weather, and other factors affect the markers and the paintballs which could result in a spike or decline in the FPS. In tournament play, markers are checked regularly throughout the day. Any player caught shooting above the field limit is eliminated and assessed with a significant point deduction penalty.

No Blind Shooting

Blind shooting is when you stick
your marker out from behind the
bunker and shoot without looking
at your target. This is disallowed
because it could result in shooting
a ref or one of your own players
unintentionally.

Bunkering

Bunkering is when you catch an opponent off guard by
sneaking up or running up to his bunker and shooting
him point blank at close range. This move, while very
common in tournament play, is often not permitted in
rec ball. Should you catch an opponent off guard in rec
ball, you are to yell loudly "surrender". If you are on the
receiving end of the move, you should immediately
raise your marker and yell "out". Any other reaction on
your part at this moment could cause you to be "lit up"
(shot many times!)

Outback Ball

Outback ball (also known as renegade or outlaw ball) is
paintball which is played anywhere other than a
commercial field. Usually in privately owned woods, a
group of players get together to have a day of fun. The
down side to this adventure is the potential for
someone to get hurt by not following the safety rules as
noted above. Without the proper supervision or reffing,
it would only take one quick lapse of judgement for
someone to get hurt, possibly seriously. A commercial
field provides the necessary environment consisting of
staging areas, separate fields with netting, chrono
stations and adequate supervision. Although I believe

anyone who is focused and plans accordingly can run a safe game, I always take the people that I want to introduce to paintball to a commercial field.

Paintball has been proven to be a safe sport when all the proper equipment is used and the games are properly supervised. There is no substitute for trained refs and a conscientious field owner, and players who put safety first.

A few additional safety tips:

Upon being shot during a game, yell "hit" as loud as possible, raise your marker above your head and walk out (or run) quickly from behind your bunker. Place the barrel plug/sock back on the marker and move off the field or to the sideline. As soon as you yell hit and raise your marker, the other players on the field should stop shooting at you. This is considered good sportsmanship.

If you are going to work on your marker in the staging area, remove all paint and air from the marker first, and unscrew the barrel from the marker prior to beginning any adjustments.

Chapter Four
Getting Started

You and a few of your friends have been talking about playing paintball for a while and have finally set the date. What do you need to do to prepare?

First off, contact your local paintball field and obtain a clear understanding of all the costs involved. (Paintball ain't cheap!) Check to see if the field accepts credit cards; many are cash only. This is important to know up front. Most fields will rent you a basic set-up (marker, mask, hopper including 100 rounds of paintballs) for around $20. They may require that you purchase field paint only when renting their equipment. The cost for this paint is usually $15-$20 per 500 rounds. Refills on air are usually around $3 per fill. The amount of air you will use and the amount of paint you will shoot will vary by the number of games you play and how aggressively you play them. First time players on the average are not very aggressive. They adapt a wait and see approach and therefore shoot less paint than those who have more games under their belt. You should allow $60-$70 in your budget for the day; of course cost will be different depending on which field you play. Bringing a group of friends with you is a good idea. You will have more fun and if you run low on paint, you can each chip in to buy paint in smaller increments to finish out the day. Most all fields sell paint cheaper by the case (2,000 rounds) than a bag (500 rounds), so factor that in on your initial purchase and partner up with your friends.

What to Bring

Always dress for the weather and, if it's cool, dress in layers. You will be moving around a lot, so you don't want to wear anything bulky or cumbersome that will restrict your movement. You also do not want to wear anything too tight fitting. Tight jeans are obviously not a good choice. Often, new players wear loose fitting clothing in an attempt to cushion them from the sting of the paintballs. I've seen numerous players show up the first time dressed like they were on their way to the Swiss Alps (and I play primarily in Florida). If you dress up like the Sta Puft Marshmallow Man or the Michelin Tire Man, you have gone way too far in your choice of attire.

Loose pants (but not too baggy) long sleeve cotton shirt and perhaps a long sleeve cover shirt will work best if the weather is not too hot. Be prepared to adapt.

For footwear, an older pair of sneakers will do just fine. All men should wear some kind of protective cup. One errant hit and you may end up singing in a higher octave for the rest of your life. Women should consider some form of chest protection. Head coverings can be as simple as a baseball hat turned backward. When wearing the goggles, the fabric of the hat works fine in cushioning your head from a hit.

Check with the field that you intend to play on as to what food and beverage items may be available. You may decide to pack a lunch. Make sure you have plenty of water and that you stay hydrated. If you are playing in the summer heat, take a break from the games as necessary to cool down.

As far as other items, I always take a spray bottle of water and paper towels or toilet paper to clean off my goggles between games. Most fields don't supply these items and its not fair to raid the fields port-a- potty. You may end up leaving someone in a real predicament.

30

The Big Day

You should arrive at the field 45 minutes to one hour prior to when you want to begin play. It takes a while to sign in, buy your paint, air up, rent your equipment, load your hopper and get ready to play.

Make sure you confirm all the costs for rentals, paint etc. If you are under 18 years old, you should be required to have a waiver form signed by your parents. Many fields are set up so that you can download this form online, have it signed, and bring it with you.

You will need to attend the field safety briefing to review all the rules and regulations for that particular field. During the briefing, **Pay Attention.** This is done for your safety (and mine) and if you break any of the rules, you probably will have to sit out a game at the least. If you have multiple offenses, you will probably be asked to leave the field with no refund. This is serious stuff!

Learn how to operate the marker you are going to be playing with. Know how to cock and de-cock the marker and how to use the safety.

Find a safe area (as designated by the field) and shoot a few balls and get familiar with the marker. Most fields have a target area just for this purpose.

If you are all checked in, have all your equipment, had your safety briefing, and are familiar with your marker, you are ready to play. Let the games begin!

Chapter Five
Beginning Basic Tactics and Strategies

When you first take the field to start the first game, the refs will divide all the players into two teams. If you wish to play with your friends, be sure to let the refs know this as soon as possible if they don't ask the group. After the teams are divided up, each team will go to their starting positions at each side of the field. At this time, all players need to formulate a basic plan. They need to agree on which bunkers they intend to take on the break and which players will be "sweet spotting". (Rapid shooting at the path just before the bunker that you expect an opponent to run for.) The objective in sweet spotting is to hopefully take out one or two of their players right off the break.

The players on your team that are not sweet spotting will be running to the key bunkers on your side of the field and will take up position there. The objective here is to take the best and farthest bunkers to the left and right (tape line or wire) and as far forward without getting eliminated. Paintball is all about gaining real estate as fast as possible and controlling the field. Taking the farthest bunkers on each tape line enables you to have better "angles" (line of fire) on your opponent. If you are able to shoot at a player behind a bunker from different angles, you can confine his maneuvering space and eventually get the elimination (pinch him out). Each time your team eliminates an opponent, the front players need to advance and the players behind him need to move up as well (fill in). Any time your team has better field position than your opponents, you are in a far better position to eliminate them. When your team has more players than their team, you will be able to put more markers on each of them, advance further down the field, and close out the game.

The other key to winning the game is staying alive. It's obviously a great move if you can make it all the way to the snake off the break. Its not so great if you get shot out on the way there. Use good judgement. Can you make it? Should you slide into the Taco at the 30 first then quickly bop into the snake? Once you make it to the snake, are you the type of player that can live there and reek havoc for a while at least? Will you be able to crawl all the way down to the end of the snake, come out and bunker their back player?

Do you have a mid or back player on your team that will communicate with you to help keep you alive? These are the types of things that you need to consider every time you play the game. Decisions must be made quickly on the field. Hesitation will get you eliminated.

Common Mistakes for Newbies

"Newbies" are players that are new to paintball. Everyone was a newbie at one time or another. Newbies are the future of paintball and deserve to be treated respectfully. I've seen many players that were newbies for 6 months to a year that are very good players today. The more experienced players look after the newer players and try to help them out. I enjoy talking to the newer players about markers and equipment, how to play better and just paintball in general. I see so much potential in these young players. I've given up many a Saturday or Sunday afternoon reffing newer players away from the mainstream players to help get them started. Here are some common mistakes beginning players make and tips on what and what not to do:

♦ **Get over the fear of getting hit.** Paintball hits do sting for a second. However, I guarantee if you get aggressive, make a few eliminations, get the blood pumping and the adrenalin rushing, you will barely feel anything.

♦ **Don't hide out in the back bunkers.** I've seen way too many players go to the nearest bunker on the break and just stay there. Barely looking out and hardly ever shooting. They can't be having much fun. Get into the game! Shoot someone before they shoot you.

♦ **Don't double up in one bunker.** Your opponents will quickly get the angles on you and then you are history. Did you ever hear the term, shooting fish in a barrel?

♦ **Shouting "HIT" too quickly.** Make sure the paint has broken before you yell hit. Feel the spot and look for paint on your fingers. You may have taken a bounce and you are not "out". Call for a paint check or ask one of your teammates.

♦ **Calling yourself out after running out of paint or air.** You should never call yourself out unless you have indeed been hit. You can still stay in the game. Fake it, distract the opponent, be the eyes for your teammates and still make a contribution.

♦ **Do not shoot repeatedly over the top of the bunker.** If you pop-up and shoot over the bunker, you are exposing yourself to all angles from the opponents side. Its like the spokes of a wheel with you at the hub. Experienced players will do this at times, but they will usually pop up and fire only 2 or 3 shots before dropping back down.

♦ **Beware of tunnel vision.** Tunnel vision occurs when a player concentrates only on one opponent and becomes oblivious to other threats, which inevitably gets them eliminated.

♦ **Learn to move.** Moving is critical to the game. Moving enables you to get in to a better position to get the angles on your opponents. When you see the side of an opponent, you can get the elimination. Often, switching bunkers will get you eliminated. However, not moving will almost always put you out of the game.

Chapter Six
Basic Skills

To become a better player, you need practice certain skills to the point where they become second nature to you. It does take a lot of practice, but all athletes do drills to keep their skills sharp. Tiger Woods just doesn't show up and play in golf tournaments. Professional baseball players have batting practice regularly and they already know how to hit. Too many newer players feel that just by playing more paintball they will get better. They will, to a degree, but it's not enough.

Be Ambidextrous

Learn to shoot left handed and right handed early on. The ability to do this well, will enable you to play any side of the field effectively. If you attempt to shoot right handed out of the left side of the bunker, you will expose too much of yourself and substantially increase the chance of being eliminated. Walk around the house holding your marker in your off hand (without paint and air of course) and get more comfortable with handling it.

Think Small

Learn how to play your bunker and stay tucked in tight. Depending on where your opponents are located and which bunker you are playing will dictate how you will play that bunker. Say you are positioned in a center lay down shooting at an opponent on the right side, you would be on both knees with the left side of your body up against the bunker. With your marker up in shooting position elbows tucked in making sure your hopper is not above the bunker, lean out the right side while shooting and come around on your target. Your profile (the amount of your body, mask, marker etc. exposed to your opponent) should always be as small as possible. Always tilt your hopper at the same angle as the side of the bunker. If you are playing a dorito out the right side, the hopper would be tilted toward the left at the appropriate angle.

Be careful when switching it up (changing to shoot from the other side) that you keep your entire body, marker and other equipment behind your prop and don't inadvertently become a target while repositioning.

When playing stand-ups, much of the same technique applies. Both feet are together while you lean out and shoot. It is advisable not to take a step out as you will expose too much of your side.

Practice positioning yourself in different bunkers from both sides and have another player look at you from an opponents bunker. How was your profile? Was your hopper tilted properly? Take your marker at home (no air or balls of course) and practice looking at a mirror while leaning out of the door way. Get the feel of bending at the waist and leaning out with elbows tucked tight.

Snap Shooting

Inevitably, you will find yourself in a situation going head to head and one on one with an opponent. When that happens, the player with the best snap shooting skills will usually come out on top. Snap shooting is simply having your marker up and ready, quickly snapping out from behind your bunker, firing only 2 or

3 balls and quickly ducking back in. This needs to be practiced on different bunkers, lay downs, as well as stand-ups and from your knees and on your feet.

You should work on snap shooting drills with a friend or a teammate regularly to become more proficient.

Sweet Spotting

As described earlier, sweet spotting is laying a string of paint in your opponents running lane just to the side of the bunker he is trying to take. This is one skill many players feel they are better at than they really are. If you are the player designated to do the sweet spotting, you will need to practice often to become really good. Holding your barrel on the board in the starting position, swing your marker around to bear on your target in one smooth direct motion and let her rip.

Shooting only a couple of balls off of the intended bunker will help you achieve the desired range, then adjust to 3 or 4 feet to the side of the bunker. Once you are on target, just keep shooting and let your opponent run in to your paint. If you master this skill and are often eliminating opponents on the break, you will be an asset to any team.

Running

Running is a little different in paintball than in other sports. The objective while running in paintball is to stay low to become less of a target. Like an Olympic runner coming out of the block, you are accelerating in a crouched position, but you never get fully upright. As you approach your bunker you are getting even lower as you prepare to slide into your bunker. Your marker should be in the same hand as the side of the field you are running to. Left run, marker in left hand. Right run, marker in right hand.

38

Sliding

You should always wear proper protective gear to slide. Sliding into bunkers can be done in several different ways. A modified baseball slide is one of the most common and is utilized mostly by mid and back players. While running to a bunker on the right side of the field, for example, you will drop down to you left side using your left hand to help guide you while sliding in. After you drop in to the bunker, pop up on your knees while switching your marker from your right hand to your left and into shooting position.

The other slide which is used primarily be front players is simply the paintball version of the "belly flop". This slide is a face first dive into your bunker. This is obviously the best slide to use for getting into the snake. When you get into the snake this way, you can continue to crawl up the bunker as far as you wish.

Diving over the top of the bunker head first to get into position is often called a "Superman" slide. When utilizing these slides, you should begin 6 to 10 feet in front of the bunker. Factoring in the condition of the field is critical in judging how early in the run you begin your slide. Obviously, if you're on a good grassy field for an 8:00 a.m. game, your slide should begin early because of the morning dew. On the flip side, if its a patchy, sandy field and you slide too soon, you will dig in and be caught in the open just short of the bunker and likely be eliminated. Experienced players often test slide bunkers when walking fields prior to the beginning of a tournament.

Shooting On The Run

Often, while sweet spotting on the break or when making a bunkering move, you will be shooting on the run. This is a skill you need to practice by holding your marker as steady as possible while making your move. Often, players miss opportunities for eliminations by not having their markers up and shooting while switching bunkers.

Chapter Seven
Basic Gear

Those of you that are new to paintball should consider playing the game several times prior to investing in all the paintball gear.

Take the time to not only make sure you have indeed caught the paintball bug, but have had the time to research what type of paintball you want to play. Do you see yourself as a scenario player, a woods player, an occasional rec ball player or a tournament player? Each style of paintball has equipment designed specifically for those individual players. It may take a little time for you to learn which style of play appeals to you the most. Find a field that offers the most variety in these styles, rent their equipment, go play and mix it up.

Read the most popular paintball magazines such as *Action Pursuit Games*, *Paintball 2 Extremes* and *Paintball Sports Magazine* to name just a few. These magazines offer a wealth of information in great detail and cover our sport very well. You can always use the internet for obtaining information on markers and accessories, but when it comes time to make the actual purchase, nothing beats your local paintball supply store and paintball fields. These individuals are very knowledgeable, have played the sport for years and are there to help you get started. They want your repeat business. When you are at the field, talk to some of the more experienced players. You will find most of them will be more than happy to answer any questions you may have to get you started.

Once you have played for a while and are ready to start purchasing the gear, do your competitive shopping. As for what equipment may be best for you, here are a few considerations:

Mask/Goggles

Paintball goggles should be your first or one of your first purchases. Goggles range anywhere from $20 to $100. Wearing a comfortable mask with good peripheral vision is very important, as your mask gets a lot of use. You will need to change the lenses when they become scratched to the point they interfere with your being able

V Force Profiler
Courtesy of Procaps

To see clearly, if a crack in the lens occurs, or if you take a pointblank lens shot. Choose goggles that have lenses that are easy to replace. Some goggles also have an optional fan that can reduce fogging for those players that wear glasses which is a nice feature. There are a lot of good goggle systems out there.

JT Proteus
Courtesy of JT USA

Some of my favorites are the JT Proteus, Dye Invision and the V Force Profiler.

Paintball markers

The paintball marker is the one piece of equipment you will most likely spend the most time researching and analyzing. There are numerous styles of markers that can fit almost any budget. Prices vary anywhere from $75-$1400 depending on how high tech you want to go. Although, the $75 to $100 markers may be fine for

42

starters or for an occasional game in the in the woods, I don't feel they are a good choice for someone who intends to play regularly. These markers, by nature, aren't as reliable and don't shoot as fast as markers in the $300 to $500 range. For this reason, don't be in a hurry to buy your first marker. Talk to

Dm5
Courtesy of DYE Precision

other players at the field, ask them if you can try their markers. This will help you determine what may be the

ANGEL
Courtesy of WDP

Intimidator
Courtesy of National Paintball Supply

best marker for you. Different markers are more appropriate for different styles of play. Spyders and Piranhas are good choices for beginners that are occasional rec ball players. Tippmans are very popular for woods and scenario games. They are rugged, reliable and have a military look to them. Tournament players like anything that shoots volumes of paint - Shockers, Impulses, Angels, Electronic Autocockers, DM5's or Intimidators are the weapons of choice. These markers are usually priced in the $1200 to $1500 range.

ION
Courtesy of Smart Parts

I personally feel that Autocockers have better distance and are more accurate than Timmys or Angels, but they are not as fast, even with E- blades or other electronics.

A lot of younger tournament players with a limited budget might invest in a Smart Parts Ion which is around $300.

When shopping for a marker in the $300 plus range, look for one with "eyes".

Eyes are electronic sensors that "see" the balls drop into the chamber before allowing the marker to shoot. This keeps you from chopping paint or pinching a ball, and jamming your marker.

Hoppers

Revolution
Courtesy of JT USA

Hoppers (the container that sits on top of the marker and holds the balls) come in many different types. A basic hopper (gravity feed) is only around $5, however you will want to upgrade to an electronic loader as you become more experienced and learn to shoot faster. You will need a hopper that can keep up. A Revolution 12 volt x board or a Ricochet are good first hoppers, although I find the Ricochet a little noisy. I used a VL Evolution II for a longtime and liked it other than having to replace the lids too often. One of the best loaders I've played with is the Empire Halo with rip drive. They are durable (as far as hoppers go) and fast. The price is $125 to $140.

Halo
Courtesy of Odyssey

Air Systems

There are basically two different types of air systems used in paintball markers. CO2 (Carbon Dioxide) or HPA (High Pressured Air). Due to the physical properties of CO2 being liquid and gas or a mixture of both, there can be significant variations in velocity that affects the accuracy of the marker. Cold weather can also adversely affect CO2. The most popular CO2 tanks come in several different sizes, the most common of which are the 7oz, 12oz and 20oz. Tanks are connected to the marker in several different ways.

Bottom Line (back bottle). The most common which is where the tank attaches to an adapter at the bottom of the grip.

Vertical Bottle. Screws into an adapter just below the barrel.

Remote System. This is where the tank is worn at the player's back, usually on a pouch in his pod back. A line extends from

CO_2 Tank

the tank to the marker. This set up has advantages for woods and scenario players. The player can use a larger tank which enables him to play longer with out having to refill. Also, with out having a tank directly attached to the marker, it is much lighter, more comfortable and easier to maneuver in tight spots.

The disadvantages are the larger tank does stick out and becomes more of a target opportunity for your opponent. The line from the tank to the marker is at times cumbersome and can get snagged in branches or bunkers. The remote line also makes switching off shooting left to right awkward.

The disadvantages make the remote system a choice I would not recommend for speedball or tournament play.

The disadvantages are the larger tank does stick out and becomes more of a target opportunity for your opponent. The line from the tank to the marker is at times cumbersome and can get snagged in branches or bunkers. The remote line also makes switching off shooting left to right awkward.

The disadvantages make the remote system a choice I would not recommend for speedball or tournament play.

__High Pressure Air__ is recommended when you can easily get fills because the velocity will be much more consistent. HPA is becoming more and more popular and is used by most all tournament players. Sizes for HPA tanks are 47cu. in./3,000 PSI, 68cu. in./3,000 PSI and 45cu. in./4,500 PSI although other sizes are available. Fills for 3,000 PSI are fairly common and available at most popular fields. However, as of this writing, the availability of 4,500 PSI is not that wide spread.

HPA Tank

When entertaining the thought of playing a different field for the first time, make sure you call ahead to confirm they have HPA. I have been to new fields only to find I had to buy air from other players since the field didn't provide HPA. These players had purchased used scuba tanks (usually $50-$60) and a fill station adapter. These are available from most paintball suppliers for around $50. With this set up you can go to most any scuba or dive shop and fill the tank for around $5. You can then fill you HPA tank approximately 14 to 18 times from the scuba tank. You will notice that as you begin to run low in the scuba tank, you will only be able to fill up to 2,000 PSI and even less as you continue to run low. Most players that use this system invest in multiple tanks. As the first tank runs low, they switch off to another tank and top off. They start with the scuba tank lowest on air and work their way up to maximize their PSI by utilizing all tanks. *Note: Only qualified persons should fill tanks. There may be dangers involved, including serious injury or death.*

I own a scuba tank set up that I keep filled in the garage. That way I always have air for when I am working on my marker and need to test it out.

Pod & Packs

Unless you are playing a game of Hopper Ball (where each player can only use the paint they bring with them in their hopper) you will need a pod. A Pod is a plastic tube holding extra rounds of paint and a Pack is a harness or belt worn around the waist with compartments (loops and straps) that hold multiple pods.

Most pods are basically the same except for a few variations. Each pod usually carries 140, to 160 rounds of paint. Pods come in a variety of colors and have snap shut plastic lids. Two of the exceptions are the Dye lock lid and the JT Slammer. The lock lid can only be opened when the button at the top is moved to disengage it. This feature greatly reduces the chances the pod will open accidentally while removing it from the pack.

4+1 Pack

Any player that has done this and dumped all their paint know how frustrating this can be (especially if it was your last pod).

47

The JT Slammer was designed for speed. It has a special lid that, when slammed in to its own specially designed hopper lid, opens like the petals of a flower, dumping all of its contents.

Packs come in many different styles and combinations. It's just a matter of which one suits your individual tastes. The pod set up in the pack is what is the most important feature. Typical combinations for packs are 4 + 1 (4 pod compartments with 1 pouch for a remote tank), 6 + 1 etc. Pack combinations such as 3 + 2 refers to 3 pod compartments with loops for 2 extra pods for a total of 5 pods. Other packs can be a straight 3 pack or 4 pack with out any other loops. The comfort of the belt is important. Some packs even have a lumbar cushion for support. I prefer the belts that have one main belt with 2 more secondary velcro straps for additional

4+3 Pack

Which set up combination is best for you depends on your style of play and you position on the field. If you are a woods or a scenario player and have a remote tank, the 4 + 1 or 6 + 1 may suit you. If you are a 5 man tournament style mid or back player, a 4 pack or 4 + 3 may be a good choice.

Again, it all comes down to which pack works best for you, depending on how you play the game. Some players simply shoot a lot of paint so when it comes down to how many pods to carry on the field, more is better.

Barrel System

One of the first items you are likely to upgrade on your marker is the barrel. A good barrel system can not only improve accuracy but it can also increase the range as well as shoot quieter.

Standard paintballs are manufactured at approximately .68 inch diameter. However, there is a small variation that can occur from batch to batch. Different manufacturers will also vary slightly on the size. In addition, the weather can also cause the paintballs to expand or contract slightly.

Freak Barrel System

Courtesy of Smart Parts

Having a barrel that is sized perfectly to the paintballs you are using on that day those weather conditions will enable your marker to perform at its optimum level. A barrel system will allow you to match the best barrel to your paint by changing the sleeves or the backs.

In 2000, the Freak was introduced by Smart Parts. Their concept was a 3 part barrel. The front piece with the parts, the back piece screws into the marker and the front piece, and the sleeve which fits into the back piece. The sleeves are interchangeable and range from small to larger. There are a total of eight sleeves that come with the Freak system so that you can select the best match for the paint you are using that day.

There are many other barrel systems on the market today that all perform well and are offered in various colors that look great with todays markers.

49

The Evil Pipe is a 2 piece barrel with 5 interchangeable backs that are different sizes without sleeves.

The Empire barrel is an interchangeable one piece system.

Protective Gear

If you are an aggressive player, there are certain items and accessories that you may want to eventually invest in to help protect yourself while playing.

Slider shorts, for one, provide extra padding at the hips and also have a front pouch or pocket that you can insert a protective cup.

Elbow to forearm pads are a good choice for any front or mid player, particularly snake players.

I also personally like the combination **shin guards and knee pads** with the velcro straps that attach from behind the calves. The knee pad cushion part is great when you are playing on your knees for any length of time. (These are a must for older players)

Most players these days wear **gloves,** to protect or cushion their fingers from a direct hit, and to protect their palms when sliding into bunkers. Many gloves are designed so that the finger tips can be cut off so as to allow better finger mobility for players to rip on the trigger.

Neck guards are neoprene strips about 1" wide that attach in the back with a velcro overlap. This would be a must for those players that want to protect themselves from the possibility of a hit to the throat area. Many players wear a scarf or bandana tied around their necks in a cowboy style to achieve the same goal.

Chapter Eight

Starting a Tournament Team

So, you've played paintball a couple of months with some of your buddies and are quickly becoming obsessed with the sport. You have bought all the gear you need. You have a reliable marker, all the basic accessories such as pods, harness, squeegees, battle swabs, electronic hoppers, paintball pants... just to name a few. You are becoming more comfortable with your game and are not afraid of getting shot. I've seen so many new players stay in the back bunkers, doing nothing to help their fellow teammates and then calling themselves out at the first sign of adversity. This is very normal for younger players and it takes a little time to get used to being shot. Lets face it, being hit by a paintball traveling 280+ FPS may hurt a little. However, the more into the game you are, the less you feel the hits. In addition, over half the shots you will take will probably be in the mask, marker or hopper and they don't feel pain.

You have been reading all the paintball magazines and have watched other tourney teams on TV or practicing at the local fields and would like to form your own team. Where do you begin?

First, find other players that have the same goals and desire to develop a team as you do. They must have the equipment and basic accessories. They also must have the time to commit to the team and the financial resources for paintballs, field fees, travel and entry fees for tournaments. Players that do not have the proper equipment or funds are not good candidates for playing on your team. These individuals will not stay with the team long and their departure will be disruptive to the overall team morale.

51

Select a team captain. This individual should be your best or your most experienced player. This individual should direct the practices and run the drills. If the average team age is 16 years or younger, I highly recommend having an adult assigned to be the team manager or coach (as opposed to Team Mom or Dad). Younger players need someone to keep things under control and properly focused. Adults must be responsible for kids on road trips. They need to help organize funds, submit entry forms, pay the fees, purchase the paint and let the players know the game schedules during tournaments.

Team Goals

The team needs to establish reasonable goals based on number of players, their abilities and financial constraints. If you are just starting out, you may want to start out forming a three man team and grow from there to a five man or even a seven man team. When playing tournaments, it's always advisable to have at least 1-2 more players on the team roster than your actual team size. This gives you the ability to substitute players from game to game should a player get tired, have equipment problems or is just having an off day. This also reduces the cost to play a tournament. If you are playing a 3 man tourney with 4 on the roster, you are dividing the cost 4 ways instead of 3. Inevitably, one teammate or another has a prior commitment on the date of a tournament, so with the larger roster you can still play.

Obviously, the downside is that each player will have less tournament playing time in addition to dividing whatever prize may be won by more players.

52

I like building a team to eight players on the roster. That gives you flexibility to play 3, 5 or 7 man. During practices you can have 3 on 3 or 4 on 4 practice games. When 3 man tournaments come up, you can field 2 teams which would increase the odds of placing in the money.

Team Practices

Practices should be run by the team captain. You need to have one person directing the activities of the practice. Team practices should be held a minimum of twice a month or every other weekend. If you are having practices only twice a month, they need to be mandatory. Everyone needs to be set up and ready to go on time. It is advisable to start with a brief team meeting. This should take only 15-30 minutes and it should be held away from other players at the field. The meeting agenda should discuss team goals and upcoming tournaments, team funds and a discussion of what to work on today at practice.

Practice drills should include snapshooting, one on ones, two on ones, bunker slides, break outs and sweet spotting... just to name a few possibilities. All players should be on the field at all times to observe and participate in any discussion even when not engaged in a drill.

One member of the team should network with other teams to set up scrimmages. Planned scrimmages with one or two other teams can be very beneficial. They make for a fun day of practice that simulates a tournament environment. It also gives you the insight to the very teams you may be up against in the future.

Practices need to be productive. Team members just showing up at a field does not a practice make. I have observed many teams hanging around the staging area, dry firing their markers to show how fast they can shoot. They stay at the field for 5 to 6 hours and play for one hour at best. I'd rather stay home and clean out the garage.

As you begin to develop your team, you will establish the different players' positions. The three basic positions in tournament style paintball are:

Front Player

This player needs to be quick, fast, and fearless. He or she must be highly skilled at snap shooting, bunker slides, and have excellent instincts and timing.

Mid Player

He has to be proficient at playing tight. The team is counting on him to be making things happen by working his way up to the fifty or the head of the snake. He needs to be prepared to bunker his opponent or do a run when the time is right. He will draw a lot of fire. It is his job to stay alive as long as possible, take out as many players as possible. If he does his job well, the attention he will attract will allow the other team players to get more kills and advance to close out the game.

The mid player needs to possess many of the same skills as that of the front player. He needs to be excellent at snap shooting, playing tight and quickly moving from bunker to bunker while staying alive.

He needs to keep the front player informed of opponent's positions on the field, the number of kills and any other changes in the game. He needs to quickly fill in when a front player advances or is eliminated.

54

Back Player

Back players need
to be skilled at
sweet spotting on
the break,
hopefully
eliminating an
opponents' or at
the least keeping
him from reaching
his primary

bunker. He may be able to keep the opposing team from
setting up on one side of the field therefore containing
the players in a smaller area and allowing his front and
mid players to be more effective.

Back players are the main source of communication
during the game calling out positions, setting up
moves, counting the kills to name a few. He also
provides suppressive fire to put in the opponents so
that front and mid players can advance. He will
advance up the field as the game progresses and will
often be the one to close out the game and hang the flag.
Back players shoot a lot of paint.

Communication

Ask any tournament player what the most important
aspect to winning a game is and they will most likely
say its the communication on the field.

It is imperative that players know where their
opponents are at all times as mentioned before. Its
primarily the responsibility of the back and mid players
to communicate this information and repeat it. All
team players need to speak the same language when it
comes to identifying bunkers or conveying any other
information.

55

Some of the common terms for bunkers on a airball field would be:

Term	Definition
Dorito	Triangle shape
Stand-up Soda Can	Upright cylindrical shape
Lay Down Soda Can, Rollie	Horizontal cylindrical shape
Brick	Rectangular cube shape
Temple	Rectangular upright w/ tapered sides
Snake	Low S shaped sometimes combined with other bunkers
Carrot	Cone shape
Tea Cups	Half sphere with wings

Dorito

Lay Down Soda Can

Snake

Now that we have the common bunker terminology, we need to position them on the field using left, right or center combined with yard markers as in football such as 30, 40 or 50. You would call out left forty lay down or right thirty Dorito. Most all tournament fields are divided in two halves with the same bunkers placed in the same position on both sides of  the field. If you hear a teammate calling out "My mirror!, My mirror!", that means there is an opponent in the same bunker on the opposite side of the field as your team mate.

Some other common field communications are:

Center standup looking at me - means the center stand up is firing at you.

Watch the left tape - means your teammate is telling you to post on the opponent at the left boundary line and expect that opponent to move.

Put him in - means shoot at an opponent's bunker to get him to duck in. This usually precludes a move by you teammate.

Switch it up - means your teammate wants you to concentrate on the opposite side of the field from where you are looking *(shooting)*.

57

Codes

An important part of communication on any paintball team is to have a predetermined set of verbal codes to further enhance the distribution of information on the field. I personally feel this is a critical aspect of the game. However, I caution newer teams to keep this list of codes small and basic for simplicity sake, at least at the beginning. During the heat of the game, players can momentarily lose their concentration and unintentionally convey the wrong information which could adversely affect the outcome of the game.

Here are a few basic codes that can be modified or expanded upon to get the job done.

Term	Definition
K	Number of kills; K2 is 2 opponents down.
50	Followed by a number representing how many players on your team are out; 51 meaning you have one player gone.
Code 7 or "7"	Reloading.
Code 9 or "9"	Marker is down or not working.
Z1	Z being the first letter of your teammate's name, 1 representing his first move after the break; back player would say Ready Z1?, then Go!, back player provides cover fire and teammate advances.

Term	Definition
Field goal	Grab the flag.
T	T followed by the amount of time left in the game; T-2 means there are two minutes left.

These are only a few suggested codes for you to experiment with on your team. The most important point is that whatever codes you establish, all players on your team need to utilize them until they become second nature.

Keeping track of what is happening on the field and communicating it to the rest of the team is paramount for success. How many times have you watched players lose track of the K count or didn't know the opponent bumped up to the Dorito and were eliminated?

Teams that are strong in communication have the edge on their opponents and win more games.

After you organize your team, start practicing and scrimmaging against other teams, you will inevitably improve your skill level and begin to win games against other teams. This will take hard work, patience, and a lot of practice. You will experience those days when your team gets "rolled" all day long. Try not to get discouraged, but learn from it. Talk to the other teams. Get input from them on how to improve your game. Soak up all the tips you can and incorporate them into your practice drills. It won't happen overnight, but if your team stays together and practices regularly, you will get better.

Chapter Nine
Playing a Tournament

Now that your team is fairly established, you may be looking to start playing tournaments. Finding out about the tournaments will be easy enough, just check the websites of all the local fields is your area.

Talk with other teams or talk with other players in your school.

Once you find a tournament you want to play, make sure all of your teammates agree and are available on that date. The next issue is the cost to play a tournament. If you are going to play a Rookie Three Man tournament a typical cost breakdown may be as follows:

Entry Fee	$150	*Per team*
All day air	$10	*Per player*
Field Paint	$80	*Per case*

Paint prices for a tournament are high as this is how monies are generated to pay for trophies and prizes. How much paint you will need will vary greatly due to the amount of paint your team shoots and how many games you play. If your team does well and makes it to the finals, you will play more games and therefore need more paint. You should probably figure on using four to five cases of paint but have money in reserve for one to two more cases if necessary. I would recommend that your paint purchase on the day of the tournament be only 2 or 3 cases initially. You can buy more paint as you need it, but having paint left over at $80 a case is not a good idea when you can buy the same paint after the tournament for $45. All team players should chip in equally to buy paint. Even though back players shoot more paint than front players, everyone contributes the same towards the "team paint".

Based on all of the above, if you have a three man roster, the total cost to play this tournament would be $167 to $223 per player. If you had a four man roster at this 3 man event, the cost would then be $127 to $167 per player.

Preparation For Play

Prior to the tournament, it's important that all players clean, service, and check all of their equipment. Change to fresh batteries in all markers and hoppers and take extra batteries with you just in case. Make arrangements to have on hand extra hoppers, a marker, tanks and anything else you can think of in case something breaks down.

 Make sure all players arrive early at the field. There is a lot to do - Captains meetings, purchasing paint, chronoing markers, etc. You need to assign one individual (not a player) to keep track of the schedule (what field and at what time), making sure everyone has reloaded their pods and aired up. This person can assist with all of the miscellaneous duties so that the players can concentrate on playing and nothing else.

It is also recommended that you assign someone to watch your equipment in the staging area at all times. Unfortunately, there is a possibility that some unscrupulous individual is out there. My team had a marker stolen at a tournament in Orlando. He found it for sale on ebay a couple of days later, contacted the police and had the individual arrested. Fortunately, the marker was recovered. My teammate was quite fortunate.

Funding Your Team/ Sponsorship

As you can see, the cost to play tournaments is quite high, especially for young players without much income. If your team is going to play tournaments regularly, you will need to be planning ahead and budgeting your funds accordingly. In the beginning, obtaining additional funds to play tournaments will be very difficult. Here are a couple of tips to get started.

Reffing at your local field or assisting at special events to earn money. You may also be able to get free paint or discounts on merchandise.

Collecting team dues. Consider collecting dues at each practice or once a month to be used for upcoming tournaments.

However, once you start saving money as a team, I highly recommend having an adult handle the funds. Also, a basic agreement should be established for disbursements of funds should a player leave the team. In my way of thinking, if a player leaves a team, on his own accord, he forfeits his dues. If the team disbands, however, all funds should be divided up between the remaining players. The status of all team funds should be reviewed at each practice. Decisions on how to use team funds should be voted on by each team member.

Discounts at Local Paintball Stores

The local paintball store where you normally purchase most of your gear and accessories may be receptive to giving your team discounts, especially if you are a good customer and refer all your friends and other players to their store. Your team should help out around the field whenever you can. Volunteer to privately ref some newer players and give them tips. Do an extra good job of cleaning up around the staging area. The owners will take notice, it sets a good example and promotes his business and he will likely remember this when you approach him for sponsorship.

Local Sponsorship

Draft a team sponsorship resume'. This could be a simple one or two page document with a team photo, a short biography with team accomplishments (if any). Any positive information such as student honor roll, volunteer work, class president, etc. is beneficial. Once this is completed, take copies to any local businesses you may frequent and solicit sponsorship money. It is obviously helpful if you know the manager personally. This is also a good time to obtain the help of a parent or other adult. They can help you approach local businesses and can also solicit their places of business for funds on behalf of your team. You would be amazed how quickly you generate money with an ongoing sponsorship program. It is imperative to send a thank you letter for all donations. Larger donations could receive a team photo signed be all players. A larger donation yet could list the business as a team sponsor on the team banner or jersey.

These are just a few ideas to get you started. However, I am sure when you all pool your ideas you will come up with many more.

Corporate Paintball Sponsorship

I would recommend that after you have placed well in several tournaments, take a shot at the big sponsorship. These companies usually reserve money for the high profile teams but you could get lucky. Start by E-mail, follow up with your team sponsorship resume' and more follow-ups there after.

I would recommend that after you have placed well in several tournaments, take a shot at the big sponsorship. These companies usually reserve money for the high profile teams but you could get lucky. Start by E-mail, follow up with your team sponsorship resume' and more follow-ups there after.

Instead of sitting around the computer instant messaging all of your friends, go to work. Divide up the prospects with your teammates. It takes a lot of work and a lot of follow up, but try not to become discouraged. Who knows? Maybe you'll land the big one.

Chapter Ten
The Dark Side of Paintball

Like any other sport, there are certain individuals in paintball that feel they must have an unfair advantage to be competitive. These players may not use steroids or a corked bat, but they find ways to get an edge by sidestepping the rules. Unfortunately, this taints the sport, and gives it a reputation it doesn't deserve.

Wiping

The most common infraction in paintball is "wiping" a hit before it is detected. I've seen some pretty innovative moves to accomplish this by players that should know better.

I saw a player at World Cup 2002 in Orlando take a hit on the hopper and proceed to wipe the paint off on the bunker while crawling to the other end. While it appeared to be a slick move, the alert ref spotted it and pulled him and another teammate.

I've seen numerous players take hits off the break and immediately drop to the ground or slide in an attempt to wipe the paint off in the dirt.

Fortunately, today's refs have seen it all. In tournament play I feel they do an excellent job in keeping the games fair.

"Illegal" markers

One of the best ways to beat your opponent is to outshoot him. To achieve this, unscrupulous players can install *"cheater boards"* or *"ramping chips"*, in their

66

markers. Some markers can also be programmed to change the *"debounce mode"*. Basically, these devices and settings enable you to shoot more than one ball per trigger pull, which can be similar to a burst or full auto mode. In most tournament play, you are allowed one ball per one trigger pull (semi-auto). Most tournaments have marker checks. If your marker is determined to have "bounce", your team will be assessed a penalty. A second offense could cause your team to be disqualified. Always check the tournament rules and play accordingly, so you don't get penalized.

Bad Sportsmanship

The one negative thing in paintball that stands out most in my mind is the **bad** sportsmanship I see on the field. I don't really see **why** some players can't control what comes out of their mouths. Why does every other word have to be an F bomb? The really sad part is that the bad language is **more** prevalent with the most experienced players.

When I attended the 2002 World Cup with my family, we watched the X Ball finals. The one pro team we came to watch was in their pre-game pump up and every other word was F-ing this and that. My wife turned to me and said, "So this is what you're exposing our son to every weekend?" I was so embarrassed. Although my wife has been supportive with all the time and money I spend on paintball, I think she would rather I go back to playing golf.

Then there's the arguing, emotional outbursts and temper tantrums that occur on the field: accusations of playing on, wiping and overshooting. All of which give a very bad impression to all the spectators consisting of mothers, fathers, brothers and sisters.

67

Keeping things in proper perspective, paintball is a high energy, adrenaline pumping sport. There is a certain amount of emotional demonstration to be expected, but players need to strive to keep their cool.

In my opinion, all field owners and tournament players need to establish standards of conduct, post these standards in writing, and enforce them. This will improve and increase their business.

Vandalism

There are stories in the news from time to time about individuals using paintball markers for random shootings and other acts of vandalism. We have to keep in perspective that its the fault of the individuals involved and not the sport that's the cause of these stupid acts. Although it does negatively reflect on our sport, it would be like blaming baseball when someone vandalizes a car with a baseball bat.

Chapter Eleven

Paintball Plays

To be successful at competitive paintball, it is necessary for a team to have a basic set of plays or opening moves planned prior to starting any game.

It is imperative to have more than one, simply due to the obvious variables that you encounter each time you play. What are the strengths and weaknesses of your team on any given day? What are the strengths and weaknesses of your opponents? What do you consider to be the key bunkers on the field you are about to play? What is your strategy for taking those bunkers and keeping your opponents out of theirs?

Walking the Field

Most of your game plan will be formulated by "walking the field." It is crucial that all team players participate in this task. Never play a field cold. You should all agree on key bunkers to take as well as who is best suited to take them. Eliminate any bunkers that you determine you can't "live in". (Stay without getting eliminated). Get down into bunkers to determine angles of fire against your opponents. Walk every bunker and let all players participate in the discussions. Consider all the "what ifs?". Take as much time as you can to analyze the field. Many games are won simply by doing a thorough job right there walking the field.

Opening Move

An "opening move" is step one of the play and is the beginning move to the first bunker position for each member of your team.

This move must be considered carefully. In a 3 man, if you lose one player on the break, you have just lost 1/3 of your team. It is more difficult to recover from a 2 on 3 in three man than it is to recover from a 4 on 5 in five man play.

All players may not agree with the various plays as outlined on the following pages; however, keep in mind that these plays are designed for newer teams as a beginning and can certainly be adapted to fit the skill levels of any team.

The emphasis here is to be organized by having a plan and executing that plan in live play. Each member of the team must be committed to the execution as laid out, even if he gets eliminated trying to reach a bunker. Should a player stop short of his goal or change the play, he will throw off the entire field balance. His teammates were counting on his support from a particular spot and if he is not there, the play will not progress as planned. There are many times, however, that your plan will end up in the toilet within the first 10 seconds of the game. In that case, the remaining teammates must adapt, fill in those positions of eliminated players and regroup. This is the time when thinking on your feet, letting your instincts kick in, and using the force may serve you well.

A couple of tips here:

At times, you will lose track of an opponent. When that happens, read your environment. Listen for markers shooting. Look for a player's shadow. Look for opponents discarding pods after reloading. Watch the refs and the spectators; they will often unintentionally give away an opponent's position.

If you are outnumbered and in a defensive mode, try to take up position in a stand up bunker; from there you will be able to see the field better and shoot out of both sides quicker than playing from your knees in a lay down.

Try a distraction; yell to an opponent you have been shooting at, "Check your hopper! Check your hopper!" Your opponent may turn his marker to check for a hit, giving you an opportunity for an elimination (you would be surprised at how many players fall for that one).

Convey misinformation; "John, your mirror shooting left!" or, "Bill, get ready to do the guy in the dorito!" Yell loudly and repeat so the other team hears. This may trick your opponents into thinking you have players in bunkers that are not really there.

If you are down to one against two, your opponents may not necessarily know this. Yell out codes and talk as if you are communicating with another teammate. This may cause your opponents to play more cautiously, buying you time to even up the score by getting an elimination or running out the clock.

Introduction to Plays

On the next several pages, we will be looking at several different plays that a team may execute during the course of a game. These plays cannot possibly depict all of the variables that can possibly occur. For these purpose of these illustrations, the opening moves by Team One will start off conservatively and step up from there on each subsequent play. Team One will always have to make their secondary bunker moves prior to Team Two, effectively keeping them in their first bunker positions. We will then walk through these plays one step at a time with the assumption that Team One has them pinned down.

The next page illustrates the field layout we will be utilizing with all of the bunkers labeled.

DEAD BOX/ STARTING POSITION

STAND UP TEMPLE

STAND UP SODA CAN

TACO

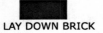

LAY DOWN BRICK

ROLLIE

DORITO

BRICK

SNAKE

ROLLIE - BRICK
(Tee)

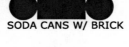

SODA CANS W/ BRICK

DORITO

BRICK

LAY DOWN BRICK

ROLLIE

STAND UP SODA CAN

STAND UP TEMPLE

TACO

DEAD BOX/ STARTING POSITION

3 Man Play Alpha

Utilizing a typical supair field layout on the attached pages we will walk through a couple of scenarios. Your team has walked this field and determined the key bunkers are the dorito and the snake. You want to occupy yours and keep your opponents out of theirs.

1. Player A takes 2 or 3 steps left (A1) and sweetspots the left 30 brick attempting to eliminate him on the break. He will only stay at this position no more than 5-7 seconds before breaking to the 40 dorito (A2).

2. Player B takes 3 steps to the right (B1) and sweetspots the lane to the left of the right 30 yard rollie.

3. Player C runs immediately for his rollie (C1) and stays for just a moment before bumping to the snake. (C2) Player B (B1) will break for the right 30 yard rollie (B2) filling in the bunker that player C has just vacated. Team 2 may not have seen the move player C made to the snake and therefore think that player B is actually player C still in the rollie.

4. Player B (B2)will now focus on keeping opponent Z pinned in his bunker while player C moves up the snake (C3).

5. Player A (A2) meanwhile is working on keeping opponent X (X1) pinned in his bunker at the 30 left brick not allowing him to advance to the left 40 dorito. This will allow player C(C1) to pop up from the snake and eliminate opponent X. (X1)

6. Player A (A2) will then put in opponent Y (Y1)at the center rear stand up and advance to the left 50 tee (A3)

7. Player B (B2) will put in opponent Z then immediately advance to the center 50, using the right stand up portion of that bunker to shield him from opponents Y and Z.

8. Once player B is in position, (B3) he will attempt to engage opponents Y and Z. Player A will advance to the opponents dorito (A4) and then eliminate opponent Y.

9. At the same time, player C will come out of the snake and do a run through(C4), first bunkering opponent Z and then continuing forward to take out player Y if he hasn't already been eliminated by player A. Player B (B3) will be ready to follow up behind player C should he be eliminated during his run through.

-Game Over-

This scenario assumes that Team One's sweet spotting was successful in containing Team Two to the middle of the field, causing them to play defensively. Once this was achieved, Team One controlled the game and executed their plan. Team One must make their secondary moves quickly to take control of the game and execute their plan.

3 MAN PLAY
ALPHA

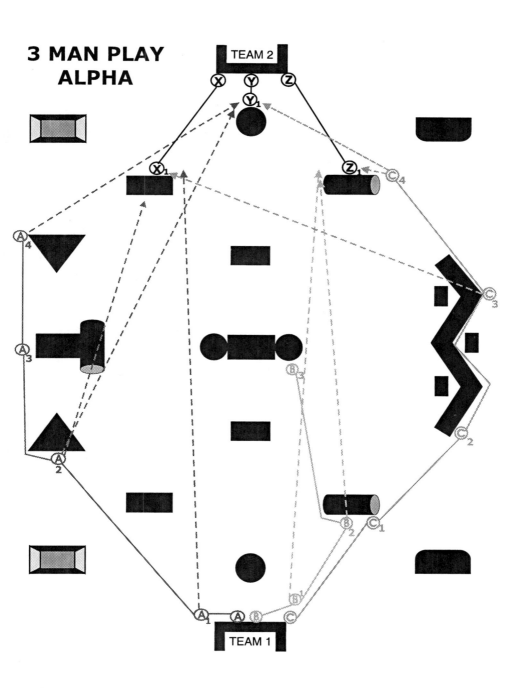

3 Man Play Beta

In this scenario, Team 2 has ascertained that their objective is also to take the dorito and the snake. Team 1 has determined to achieve their objectives, they are going to step up the pace.

1) Player A takes 2 or 3 steps to the left, sweet spotting the lane to the back left temple. (A1) He will continue for only 3-5 seconds before breaking for the left dorito. (A2) He will run low and fast expecting heavy fire from opponent Y in the rear center stand up.

2) Player C will go directly into the snake off the break. (C1) Player B will take two steps to the right and sweet spot the lane between the right rear taco and the 30 yard right rollie confining player Z to that right rollie effectively keeping him out of the snake.

3) Player B moves to his rollie (B2) to protect player C as he moves up the snake (C2) by staying posted on opponent Z in the right 30 rollie.

4) Player A (A2) will to pound the left side of the left rear temple forcing player X (X1) to look right. Player C (C2) will pop up and eliminate opponent X.

5) Player A (A2) will bump to the 50 tee (A3) while player B (B2) bumps to right side of the center 50 (B3).

6) Player A (A3) will run through left side past dorito (A4) and eliminate opponent Y.

7) Players B (B4) and C (C4) will run through and eliminate opponent Z (Z1) or opponent Y if he happened to survive the move from player A (A4)

-Game Over-

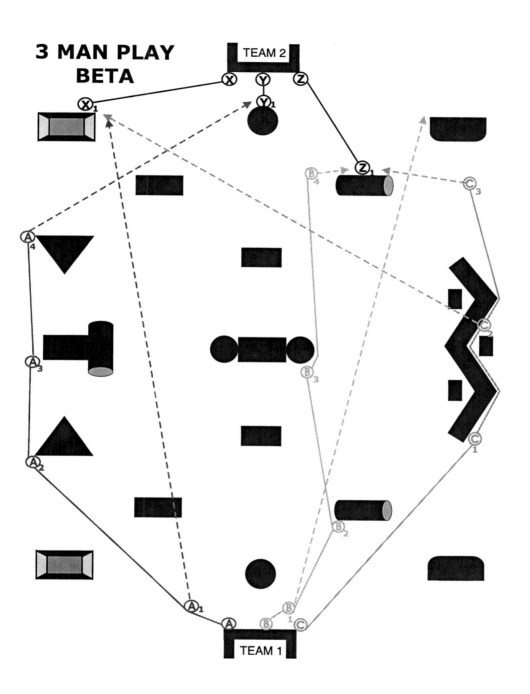

3 MAN PLAY
BETA

3 Man Play Delta

This is an aggressive play which involves shooting on the runwhile moving far up field right off of the break. It is risky and it is fairly likely that you will lose a player on the break, however, if your opening move is successful, your team will be in an excellent position to win the game.

1) Player A will sweetspot the lane between the left 30 brick and the left dorito and then break to his left 40 dorito (A1). Player A will engage opponent X (X1) (assuming he was not eliminated on the break) as well as trade paint with opponent Y (Y1).

2) Player B runs up the middle sweetspotting the lane between the right rollie and the snake, confining opponent Z (Z1) and not allowing him to reach the snake. Player B will run all the way up to the right side of the center 50 (B1).

3) Player C will make a run past the rollie while shooting the lane between the center rear stand up and the right 30 rollie. Once player C (C1) dives in to the snake, he will immediately advance to the second brick (C2).

4) Player B (B1) will put in opponent X (X1) distracting him long enough for player C (C2) to pop up and get the elimination.

5) Player B (B1) will then pound opponent Y (Y1) on the left side of the center rear stand up allowing player A (A1) to bump up to the right 50 Tee.(A2)

6) Players A (A2) and B (B2) will attempt to pinch out player Y (Y1). Player A (A2) can further advance to A3 and eliminate opponent Y (Y1) from there.

7) Player C (C2) will move down the snake and come out to the right 30 rollie (C3) and bunker opponent Z (Z1).   *- Game over -*

3 MAN PLAY
DELTA

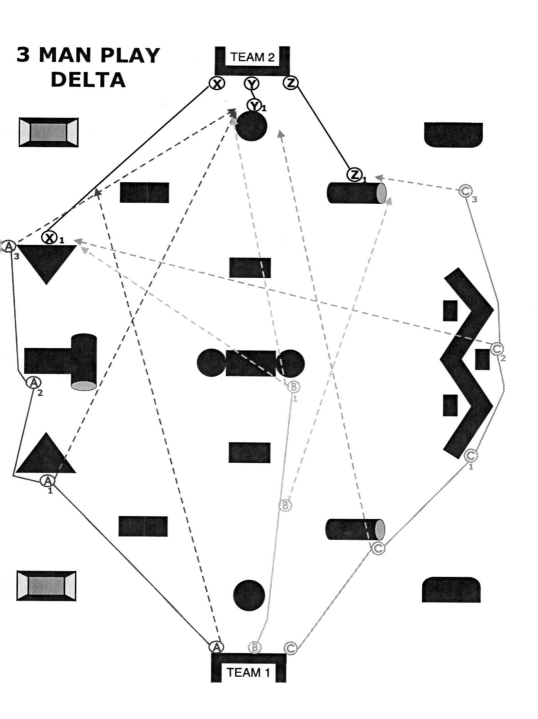

TEAM 2

TEAM 1

5 Man Play Alpha

In this scenario, Team One is executing a traditional 5 man conservative opening move. Although this will favor them reaching their initial bunkers without losing any players, it places them in a more defensive game should Team Two play more aggressively.

1) Player A immediately goes to his back temple (A1) while player E goes directly to the back taco (E1). Player B steps out to B1 while sweetspotting the lane to the right side of the left 30 brick and then drops into the 30 brick (B2).

2) Player C sweetspots the lane between the left rear temple and the left 30 brick. Player D steps out to D1 and sweetspots the lane between the right 40 rollie and the right rear taco before taking up position in his rollie (D2).

Once Team One players have all reached their starting bunkers, they will cross it up and begin shooting their opponents on the opposite sides of the field.

3) Player A (A1) will work on opponent Y (Y1), player B (B2) will work on opponent Z (Z1), player D (D2) will work on opponent V (V1), and player E (E1) will take on opponent W (W1).

4) Center stand up player C will concentrate primarily on the right side of the field to keep opponents Y (Y1) and Z (Z1) from bumping up to the snake. He will also look left side now and then to put in opponent W (W1) and keep him from advancing to the left dorito.

5) Player A (A1) will advance to the left dorito (A2). He will focus on and eliminate opponent Y (Y1).

6) Back player E (E1) shoots in opponent W (W1) to allow player D (D2) to bump into the right snake (D3).

7) Player D will advance up the snake to D4. He will pop up and eliminate opponent W (W1) and then go to work on opponent V (V1). Player E (E1) will constantly watch tape side to protect Player D from being bunkered.

8) Player A (A2) will advance to the left 50 Tee (A3). If players A (A3) and D (D4) successfully reach their positions after eliminating opponents W and Y, player A (A3) will work on opponent X for the elimination. Player D (D4) will advance to D5 and will snap out opponent V (V1).

9) Player B (B2) will advance to the left side of the center 50 (B3) and player C will advance to the right side (C1). He will be looking at Y1 and Z1, keeping them contained.

10) Player D (D5) will do a run through and bunker opponent Z (Z1) with support from A (A3) and B (B3) to close out the game.

- Game Over -

It is imperative in this game that Team One make their secondary moves quickly to put Team Two in a defensive mode. Waiting too long could change the outcome completely.

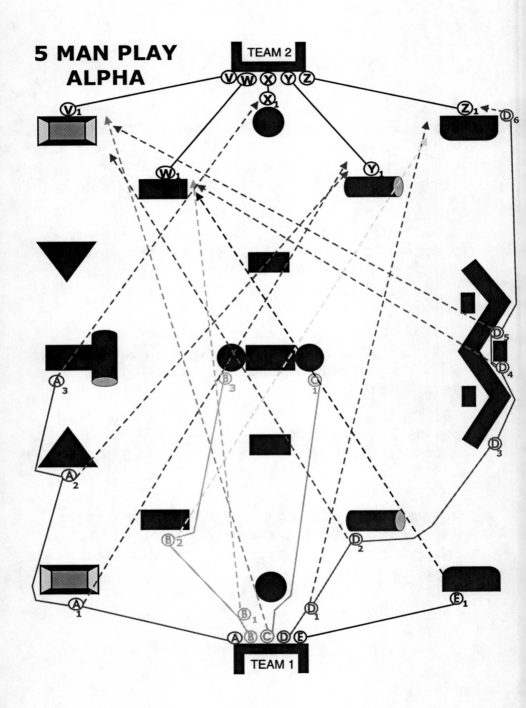

5 MAN PLAY
ALPHA

5 Man Play Beta

In this play, Team One will play a little more aggressively by sending their wing men further up field on the break. This is a little more risky, but they are more likely to control the game early on.

1) Player A will go to the left 40 dorito (A1) on the break, and player E will dive into the right snake (E1).

2) Players B (B1), and D will sweetspot one lane left side and one lane right side in an attempt to eliminate one or two opponents or, at the least, confine them to the rear bunkers, while Player C advances to the center 50 left side (C1).

3) Player B (B1) will break to the left 30 brick (B2) after 5 to 7 seconds. Player D will drop into the right 30 rollie, again after 5 to 7 seconds of sweetspotting (D1).

4) Player A (A1) will go to work on opponent X and Y (Y1), whichever proves to be the best target. Chances are he will probably eliminate opponent Y (Y1) first.

5) Player E (E1) will move down the snake to E2 and pop up and eliminate opponent W (W1).

6) Players A (A1) and E (E2) can then both go to work on opponent X, effectively pinching him out for the elimination.

7) Player C (C1) will team up with player A (A1) shooting tape side and eliminate opponent V (V1).

8) Player A (A1) will bump up to the left 50 Tee (A2) and shoot across field at opponent Z (Z1). Player C (C1) will also look inside to opponent Z (Z1) and player E (E2) can then come out of the snake (E3) to bunker opponent Z (Z1) and close out the game.

- Game over -

83

5 MAN PLAY
BETA

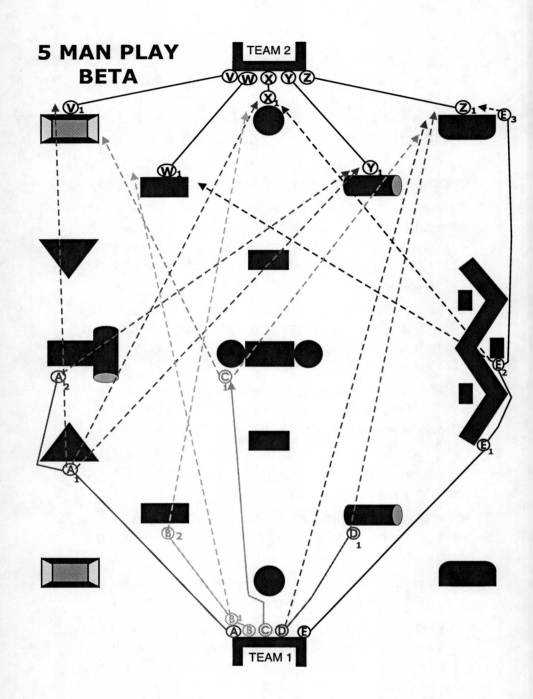

5 Man Play Delta

This is a very aggressive five man play. It requires players to shoot on the run, drop into their bunkers quickly, and gain control of the field right off the break. It is also very risky. (Some would even say suicidal.) If you drop one or two players at the start, your team could quite easily lose the game. However, if all the players make it to their first bunkers, your opponents will go into a "what's happening" mode as you have just cut the playing field in half. Your entire team is now on their turf and in their face.

1) Player A goes directly to the left 40 dorito (A1), and then immediately bumps to the left 50 Tee (A2).

2) Player B sweetspots the lane between the left rear temple and the left 30 brick on the run and all the way to the left side of the center 50 stand up (B1 & B2).

3) Player C sweetspots the lane between the 30 right rollie and the right rear taco on the run all the way up to the right side of the center 50 stand up (C1 & C2).

4) Player E goes deep into the snake off the break (E1). Player D sweetspots his lane between the right 30 rollie and the center rear stand up briefly before dropping into his right 30 rollie (D1). He the quickly bumps into the snake with player E (D2).

5) Player E (E1) pops up and eliminates opponent X at the center stand up and then moves up to E2.

6) Player D has moved up to D3 where he pops up and eliminates opponent W (W1).

7) Players A (A2) and B (B2) eliminate opponent Z (Z1).

8) Players C (C2) and E (E2) eliminate opponent V (V1).

9) Player E (E2) comes out of the snake and bunkers opponent Y (Y1).

- *Game over* -

This play enabled Team One to put two shooters on nearly every opponent to get the eliminations. This was because they took so much of the field so quickly that they had all of the angles before Team Two really knew what was happening. Team One had to simply wait and pick them off one by one.

5 MAN PLAY DELTA

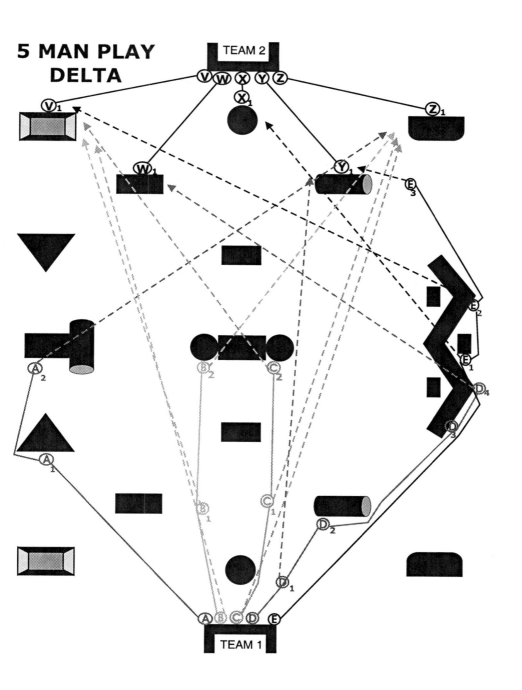

TEAM 2

TEAM 1

87

Glossary

Airball	Paintball played on fields with inflatable bunkers made by companies such as Sup'Air.
Agitator	The propellor or wheel in an electronic hopper that helps feed the balls into the marker.
Air system	The air system is all the items that flow the air or hold the air.
Battle Swab	A stick with a fluffy swab at both ends. It can be folded in half and placed in the pants side pocket for field use.
Bonus ball	Unsportsman like extra hits on a player that has been eliminated.
Bunker	A prop or structure on the field used for cover. Also a move where you run up or sneak up on an opponent and shoot
Bump	A move to the next bunker to advance down field.
Breaking Paint	Also known as chopping paint, this is when a ball breaks inside the marker. This can happen for several reasons.
Break	(Or break out) The opening move in a game. All players start at opposite ends of the field with barrels on the board or in a start box(deadbox).
Chrono	To check the velocity of a paintball marker using a chronograph; a chrono is a device for checking the speed of a paintball as it leaves the barrel of a marker measured in feet per second. (FPS)

Compressed Air	HPA, High pressure air, N2, nitro. A power source used in paintball.
Fill in	The move to another bunker that was vacated by your teammate while moving up field.
Hit	Anytime a ball breaks on you or any part of your equipment that leaves a splat the size of a quarter or larger.
Hopper	A container that sits on top of the marker that holds the paintballs, also called a loader.
Mirror	Usually refers to the same bunker location at the exact opposite side of the field from where you are playing.
Paintcheck	Asking a referee to verify you or your opponent have been hit. You may also ask a fellow player.
Pod	Cylindrical shape tube with snap shut lids that usually holds about 140 paintballs.
Post	To aim directly at the spot where you anticipate an opponent to pop out from behind his bunker to shoot; Stay posted on that dorito!
Put in	To shoot at an opponent's bunker so that he tucks back in. This is often done just prior to changing bunkers or any other offensive move.
Reg	Regulator; regulates amount of air going in to markers.

Run through	When a player comes out of his bunker, shooting on the run while attempting to eliminate one or more opponents.
Splatter	Paint residue on a player or his equipment after a paintball has struck another object first. Usually not considered a hit.
String	Rapid shooting in a straight line that almost resembles a string of pearls.
Sweet spotting	Rapid firing at a spot just outside a bunker that an opponent is running for, hoping to eliminate him on the break.
Squeegee	A device that is pulled through a barrel of a marker to clean out paint or dirt.
Tape	The left or right side boundary line of the field.
Timmy	Slang for a Bob Long Intimidator.
Velocity	The speed at which a paintball travels measured in feet per second.
Wiping	Cheating by wiping off a paintball hit.

Ready for Action

Making it Happen

Last Minute Instructions

Taking Care of Business

Ready or Not

They're Off

The Waiting Game

You're Mine

Show Me The Money

Men at Work and the LA Exodus Kids

Larry Sekely and daughter Jessica

Paintball 102

The Next Step:
Developing a Tournament Team

By Larry Sekely

About the Author

Larry Sekely works and lives in the Tampa bay area with his wife of nineteen years, Barbara, his son, Jason, age sixteen, and his daughter, Jessica, age thirteen. He was introduced to paintball by Jason, who was ten at the time, shortly after attending a friend's birthday paintball party at a local field. Over the next several years, Larry and his son played paintball in all their spare time and eventually began to participate in local tournaments.

In the summer of 2003, they formed Team ICE with a couple of Jason's friends. By the summer of 2004, the team had grown in size and skill level and had finished at the top in tournaments in Miami, Port Canavaral, as well as Tampa, Florida.

Team ICE disbanded shortly after the tragic death of it's co-captain, Chris Hidalgo, in July 2004.

Larry currently plays for "Men at Work", a team comprised of the fathers (and in one case the grandfather) of younger paintball enthusiasts. The team has a minimum age requirement of 40 years old.

Printed in the United States
139082LV00011B/242/A